GO ▶ golf

Gavin Newsham

London, New York, Munich, Melbourne, Delhi

Project Editor **Nicky Munro**
Project Art Editor **Jenisa Patel**
DTP Designer **Vania Cunha**
Production Controller **Melanie Dowland**
Managing Editor **Stephanie Farrow**
Managing Art Editor **Lee Griffiths**
Photography **Gerard Brown**

Produced for Dorling Kindersley by
XAB Design, London
Design **Beverley Speight, Nigel Wright**
Editorial **Liz Dean**

DVD produced for Dorling Kindersley by
Chrome Productions
www.chromeproductions.com
Director **Robin Schmidt**
Camera **Neil Gordon**
Production Manager **Portia Mishcon**
Production Assistant **Jolyon Rubinstein**
Voiceover **Robin Schmidt**
Voiceover Recording **Mark Maclaine**
Music by **Scott Shields**, produced by **FMPTV**

First published in Great Britain in 2006
by Dorling Kindersley Limited
80 Strand
London WC2R 0RL

A Penguin Company

2 4 6 8 10 9 7 5 3
002 - GD061 - Nov/10

A CIP catalogue record for this book is available from
the British Library.

ISBN: 978-1-4053-6320-4

Colour reproduction by Icon Reproduction, UK

Printed and bound by Hung Hing in China

scover more

om

contents

how to use this book and DVD

This fully integrated book and accompanying DVD are designed to inspire you to get out onto the golf course. Watch all the essential techniques on the DVD in crystal-clear, real-time footage, with key elements broken down in state-of-the-art digital graphics, and then read all about them, and more, in the book.

Using the book

Venturing onto the course for the first time can seem a daunting prospect, so this book explains everything you need to know to get you started with confidence. Cross-references to the DVD are included on pages that are backed up by footage.

Switch on the DVD
When you see this logo in the book, check out the action in the relevant chapter of the DVD.

Using the DVD

Supporting the book with movie sequences and computer graphics, this DVD is the perfect way to see key techniques demonstrated in precise detail. Navigate to each subject using the main menu, and view sequences as often as you like to see how it's done!

Flick to the book
When you see this logo on the DVD, flick to the relevant pages of the book to read all about it.

why play golf?

Golf is more popular now than it has ever been. Thanks to the popularity of professional players such as Tiger Woods and Michelle Wie, the game has grown to such an extent that there are now an estimated 60 million golfers in the world, playing on some 32,000 courses. It's a truly global game – from Australia to the Zambia, you are never far from a golf course. Even in countries not traditionally associated with the game, the golf bug has bitten. For example, the People's Republic of China now has around 200 golf courses and thousands more are planned for the next decade.

The game may be so popular because it offers something for everyone. For teenagers to pensioners, golf can be challenging and intense, fun and frustrating. It's a game in which honesty and integrity are every bit as important as your proficiency level, and it remains one of the few sports in which, thanks to the handicapping system, players of all standards can compete on equal terms. The fact that the beginner can take on the professional and win makes golf perhaps the most democratic game of all.

Once you begin playing, you will soon realize that golf is one of the most addictive and absorbing sports there is. From that putt that nearly dropped to the soaring shot that split the fairway, it can also be one of the most rewarding. It is, moreover, about a shared experience, about enjoying the company of your fellow players and reliving the highs and the lows of your round, the good shots and bad. Just don't be surprised if you get hooked.

go for it

coming up...

the object of the game

The object of the game is simple – just get the ball into the hole in as few shots as possible. However, a golf course presents a variety of challenges, and you will need to practise your techniques to bring down your score.

You'll find that most golf courses consist of nine or 18 holes. Each hole is allocated a "par" rating, or the ideal number of shots needed to complete that hole. The longer the hole, the higher the par. So for a par-four hole, you should be trying to finish it in four shots or fewer. If it's a par-three, then it's a shorter hole requiring three shots or fewer, and so on. A par for the course is the total of each hole's par combined. Most 18-hole courses have a par that is between 68 and 73.

Keep in mind...

- As a beginner, you won't have to worry about your par rating. Only extremely good players come close to shooting par or better for their round.

- Concentrate your efforts on the fundamentals of the game, such as your swing and posture.

- When you do play a round, try to anticipate the potential problems of each hole to reduce the possibility of making unnecessary mistakes. Do this, and your scores will soon start to come down.

types of play

From fourballs to foursomes, from Stableford to Texas Scramble, there's a multitude of games you can play. Whether you prefer to play with one partner or as part of a team, there is a game out there to suit you.

All you need to remember is that, essentially, there are only two types of competitive golf – stroke play and match play. Most other golf games are variations on these. Whatever format you choose to play, the primary objective of any game of golf is to have fun – so get out there and enjoy yourself.

Stroke and match play

• Stroke play (also known as "medal play") is a game where the lowest total number of strokes for one round, or a pre-arranged number of rounds, determines the eventual winner. In other words, the lowest score wins.

• The original form of golf competition, match play, differs to stroke play in that each individual hole is a contest in itself and the team or player winning the most holes, rather than recording the lowest total, is deemed to be the winner of the game.

observing the rules

While the official rules of the game are laid down jointly by the Royal and Ancient Golf Club of St Andrews, Scotland and the United States Golf Association, the beauty of golf is that is largely self-regulating.

While players are expected to play to the rules at all times, they must also admit to any infringement and accept the relevant penalty. Even if you're not familiar with every rule in the R & A's 192-page book Rules of Golf (and few people are) you must always play with consideration, honesty, and integrity, not merely for benefit of your fellow players but also for the benefit of the golf course. As it says in the Rules of Golf: "Play the ball as it lies, play the course as you find it and if you can't do either, do what is fair..."

a Get your clubs
You are allowed to take a maximum of 14 golf clubs out on to the golf course. There is no minimum amount of clubs you must carry in your bag.

b Getting out of trouble
When the ball doesn't go quite where you intended it to go, you'll need to know exactly what you are entitled to do when it lands in water, a hedge, or in a bunker – see pages 126–27 for the techniques you'll need to get out of trouble.

c Play it as it lies
This is the basic tenet of playing golf and, although there are a few exceptions, adhere to it at all times. The only place where you are permitted to pick up the ball is on the putting green, and only if you mark it beforehand.

d Gear up
Before you head to the golf course, first think about what you are going to wear. If you're in any doubt about what to choose, stick to the simple attire of a collared shirt, sweater, and trousers or a skirt, but not jeans.

anatomy of a golf course

Your first visit to golf club can be an intimidating experience, but when you begin to recognize all the different features of the course and understand their function, you'll enjoy new feelings of familiarity and confidence.

If at any point you're unsure about where you are – and what you can and can't do – on the golf course, ask for assistance. Other players will always prefer you asking for advice rather than going ahead and getting it wrong. Here's what you can expect to encounter on the course.

⌐ The range
Most good golf courses will have a practice ground, also known as the "range", where you can loosen up before you begin your round (see pages 134–35). Make sure that you take advantage of it.

b Sand trap
Bunkers, or sand traps, are course hazards, and come in all shapes and sizes. They can be found on the fairway (such as the one shown here) or surrounding the putting green.

⌐ The putting green
The putting green is where the hole is located. The grass here is very short compared to that on the rest of the course.

d The rough
If your ball goes awry you may find yourself in what's known as the "rough". Try to avoid it, as escaping from the rough may prove difficult (see pages 124–25).

e The teeing ground
Often called "the tee", the teeing ground is where you will play your first shot on each hole.

furniture of the course

When you first navigate your way around a golf course, you'll come across a variety of unfamiliar things that seem to make no sense whatsoever. However, each pole and post, each marker and marking is there for a reason. It may be denoting a hazard or telling you how far you have to go to the putting green, but even if you're not entirely clear about what it means, there's no need for concern. You're not expected to know the purpose of everything on the course before you play. Enjoy your golf first and learn as you go along.

a Buggies
Buggies are a fun way to get around the course. Just be sure to stick to the designated routes.

b Flags
Some flags have markers on them to denote where the hole is positioned on the green. If the round marker is at the top of the pole, it means that the hole is located towards the back of the green. If it is near the bottom of the pole, the hole is at the front of the green.

c Distance markers
Distance markers are located on the fairway or at the side of the fairway. They tell you the distance you have to go before you reach the putting green.

d Holes
The hole is where you're trying to put your ball – getting the ball into the hole is known as "holing out." Found on the putting green, the diameter of every hole measures 10.6 cm (4¼ in).

c

d

go get kitted out

coming up...

Clubs: 32–35

A lowdown on the essential clubs – the woods, irons, and putters – that you'll need to get started, plus what to look for when choosing them.

Golf balls and accessories: 36–39

Two-piece, three-piece, multi-layered, high-spin, or low spin – which ball should beginners really be using? Here's a guide to making the right choice, plus what you need to know about choosing accessories, from a golf bag to a towel and tee pegs.

What to wear: 40–45

Today's golf gear is designed for both comfort and practicality, along with stylish accessories to complete your on-course look. Find out, too, what not to wear on the course.

Weighted clubface

The clubface of this iron has what's called "perimeter weighting." This is designed to be more forgiving than other clubs, and help lessen the effects of badly hit shots.

Shaft

Beginners should look for clubs with steel or graphite shafts. Both have their merits, so you should always try before you buy.

Clubface grooves

The grooves on the clubface of this iron help to bite the ball on impact, making it spin and keeping it in the air longer. Be sure to keep grooves free of dirt.

Cavity backing

Cavity-backed clubs like these have a larger sweet spot than other clubs, making them easier for beginners to use.

choosing clubs

Buying your first set of golf clubs can be a daunting experience, not least because there is a truly bewildering array of clubs available that cater for every standard of player and every budget. As a beginner, look for a club that is geared towards the novice and offers ease of use and forgiveness on those shots that don't go to plan. You may want to consider buying a half set (typically consisting of two woods, five irons, and a putter) and build up to a full set once you're happy with the clubs. Think also about booking yourself in for what's called a "custom fit" with your local golf shop professional. This will help you find the right club for your standard of play.

Fairway wood

This fairway wood has a smaller head and a shorter shaft than a driver, and is much easier to use than its larger cousin.

Lofted face

The fairway wood is popular with beginners because it has a more lofted face and offers greater control than the driver.

Driver

A driver has a wide, shallow face. The least lofted of all the clubs, it is designed to propel the ball the greatest distance.

Club covers

Covering your driver, fairway woods, and your putter with club-head covers can save them from unnecessary damage. These clubs are generally the most expensive ones in a player's set and therefore need extra protection when they are rattling around in your bag.

putters

Of all the clubs in a golfer's bag, the putter is loved and loathed in equal measure. When things go right on the green and the putts are dropping from all distances, it becomes the club that you simply can't live without. But when things go wrong, as they inevitably do, it all too often becomes the scapegoat, discarded in the next round in favour of a different model.

Many beginners find that what's called a "heel and toe" putter is the easiest to use, but before you settle on one, take a selection on to a practice green and hit some putts. Most golf clubs will allow you to try putters before you buy them (you can ask at the club shop). Some will feel great, some a little awkward, some light, and others heavy. It's a question of feel, and you will only find out what feels comfortable by experimenting.

The putter in action
Notice how the head and the face of the putter differs to that of other clubs. The reason that the putter has an angled kink in the neck is to keep it parallel to the green, ensuring a smoother putting stroke and a better roll. The face has virtually no loft, so that the ball hugs the green on its way to the hole.

a Heel and toe putter
These putters are best suited to the novice golfer as they have a bigger sweet spot and offer greater forgiveness on mis-struck putts.

b Sight lines
Some putters have sight lines on the head to help give you a better chance of striking the centre of your ball during your putting stroke.

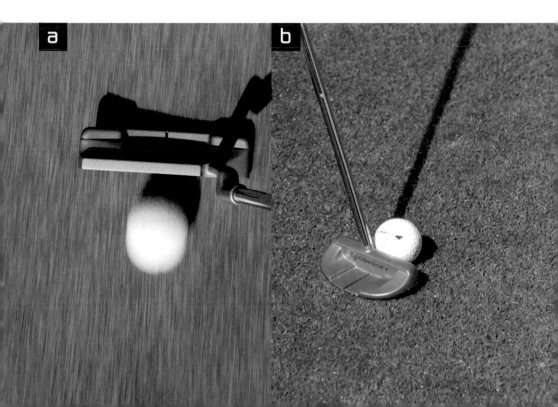

choosing balls

A golf ball's a golf ball, right? Wrong. They all may look alike, but there are dozens of different types of ball available, ranging from soft core to liquid core, low spin to high spin, cut-price to prohibitively expensive. But how do you choose the right one for your golf game?

Know your balls

• Beginners and moderate handicappers often prefer to use a 2-piece Surlyn covered ball. These balls are the most popular as their low spin rates offer greater distance while minimizing the effect of slicing and hooking (see pages 100–01).

• If you're looking for greater control on your shots and higher spin rates, you'll need a softer ball. Balata balls (so-called because they're coated in a rubber-like substance called balata) may cost you in distance, but they offer much greater control than a standard 2-piece ball. However, they do have a high spin rate, which has the knock-on effect of exaggerating any slice or hook – and is therefore suitable for more experienced players.

• Whatever ball you use you must keep it clean, as dirt will affect the quality of the contact with the clubface. Use the ball-washers usually found next to the tee box, and when you're on the green be sure to mark your ball, pick it up, and wipe it.

golf accessories

You've found a set of clubs you like and you're itching to get out there and try them, but you'll need more equipment before you play a round. You'll need golf shoes (see pages 42–43) and a golf bag to carry your clubs in – most golf clubs will insist you have these items before you play.

Next, get the little things that make the game so much easier: tee pegs for those all-important tee shots, a ball marker for marking your ball on the putting green, a pitch mark repairer, a towel, and, depending on when and where you're playing, lightweight waterproof clothing and an umbrella.

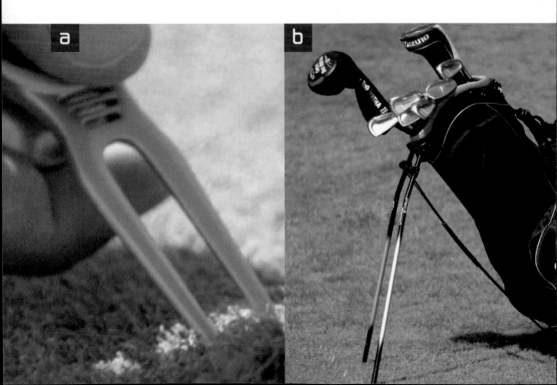

a Pitch mark repairer
This is a small but vital accessory. It is used to make good any damage your ball causes to the putting green when it lands.

b Golf bag
There's a variety of bags on the market, from super-thin pencil bags to remote-controlled trolleys. A safe bet for a beginner is this type of lightweight, durable stand bag.

c Golf towel
Use your towel for cleaning your clubs after your shot, and to wipe golf balls before teeing off. Keeping clubs and balls dirt-free improves their performance.

d Umbrella
Larger and sturdier than most standard umbrellas, many golf umbrellas also have an "anti-flip" wind-resistant canopy, invaluable for the exposed conditions of the golf course.

golf clothing

a

b

c

d

e

Of all the preconceptions that exist about the game of golf, it is players' clothing that has perhaps inspired the most heated conversation.

Remarkably, however, no dress code is stipulated in the rules of the game, and any decision about what you can and can't wear on a particular golf course rests with each individual golf club. However, it's generally accepted that you should never wear jeans or trainers, and that a shirt with a collar is always preferable to one without.

Thankfully, though, the days of pastel shades and dubious knitwear are long gone. Now some of the most stylish brands in fashion are moving into golfwear, creating clothes that are both fashionable and practical – so much so that there really is no excuse for being badly dressed on the golf course.

Gloves
Made from leather or synthetic fabrics, golf gloves are available in all sizes and a range of colours, and are designed to give you a better grip on your club.

Caps
Baseball-style caps and sun visors are invaluable for keeping the sun out of your eyes when you're playing.

Wristbands
Fast becoming a mainstay of golfwear, wristbands provide support and comfort for the wrists, helping with swing.

Women's wear
As well as shorts and trousers, women have the option of wearing a skirt, which may have a split for ease of movement.

Polo shirts
The classic polo shirt is popular golfwear. Comfortable, loose, and easy to swing in, it is also smart enough to wear on any golf course.

Basic benefits

The modern golf shoe is lightweight, durable, and waterproof.

Spikes

The spikes on the sole of golf shoes provide a better grip in all weather conditions.

Uppers

Leather uppers allow the feet to breathe while still providing protection against the elements.

golf shoes

Heel

The heel helps absorb some of the shock produced as you swing. They often have extra padding to aid stability through the shot.

Instep

Most modern golf shoes are designed to provide valuable support for the mid-section of the foot.

Padding

Comfort is crucial. Look for generous padding around the heel, which reduces friction that can lead to blisters.

During an average round of golf you will walk more than 8km (five miles) so it's imperative that you have the right footwear for the task ahead.

A pair of good-quality golf shoes will make your rounds much more comfortable and provide you with a solid foundation, allowing you to swing the golf club without the fear of losing your balance.

Like most golf equipment, the golf shoe has evolved. Players no longer wear the sharp metal spikes of old – instead, soft spikes or "cleats" (see right) have become widely fashionable.

the beginners' kit

Before you begin playing golf, it's a good idea to assemble an outfit that you not only feel comfortable in, but which complies with the club's dress code. That means a pair of non-denim trousers or skirt, a collared shirt, and a pair of golf shoes with soft spikes. But if you're still not sure what is acceptable on the golf course, call the club to check.

Look the part
A dress code doesn't mean that clothes have to be dull. Now, as the popularity of the game spreads, there are more fashionable brands in the golfwear market than ever before.

Dress for the heat
When playing in warm climates choose clothing in lightweight cotton to keep cool on the course. Wear a hat and apply sunscreen regularly for sun protection.

Waterproofs
You'll need a waterproof jacket and trousers for those days when the weather turns bad. They should fit so that you can still swing freely while wearing them.

Hats
You can buy golfing hats from specialist golf retailers, but it's fine to wear any baseball-type hat on the course.

Shirts
A shirt with a collar such as this will be acceptable at most golf clubs.

Gloves
Buy proper golf gloves, since they are specially designed to improve your grip. Breathable fabric keeps your hands comfortable and dry.

Shorts or trousers
Never wear jeans on the golf course. Shorts should always be knee-length and tailored.

Shoes
Apart from your clubs, your shoes are the most important item in your kit – so buy the best you can. Most courses do not allow trainers

go get started

coming up...

The golf swing can be an intimidating prospect for beginner players.

Trying to combine the various elements of the swing in to one fluid movement may seem hard enough, but to then propel a small ball hundreds of yards into the distance may appear virtually impossible. However, when you understand the core dynamics of the golf swing, you'll soon learn to hit the ball with confidence.

start with the swing

Elements of the swing

- If you want to swing well, you'll need to get the basics right. That means mastering the all-important issues of posture, set-up, aim, and alignment.

- Focus on movement – see just how your body should be moving throughout the swing sequence.

- Understand the vital stages of the swing, from the takeaway to the follow-through, and practise until you get all of them right.

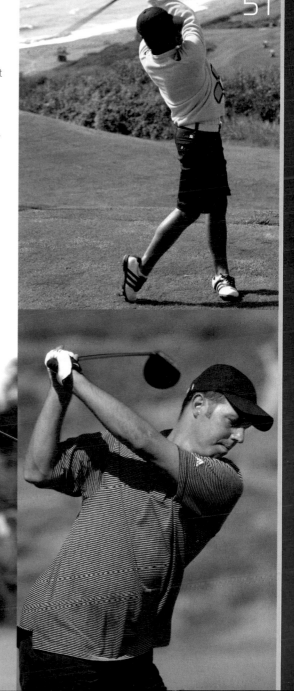

swing posture

Maintaining a proper posture before, during, and after you hit the ball allows you to make a better, more efficient swing, so it's important that you get into the habit of setting yourself up correctly. Get it wrong and you'll lose both accuracy and distance. Get it right, and you'll soon achieve the consistent swing you're aiming for.

1 A key factor in producing a reliable golf swing is your body position, which needs to be right at the very start. First, take a 7-iron and stand over the ball with your legs shoulder-width apart. Remember that the width of your stance differs depending on what club you use.

2 Don't stand too far away from the ball. Your arms should hang down and not be stretched out. You also need good balance to swing and then accurately return the centre of the clubface to the centre of the ball, so make sure that your weight is evenly distributed over both feet.

3 Try not to lean forward too much, or your swing will shorten and you'll lose power. When your posture is right, the top of your spine, the tips of your elbows, your knees, and the balls of your feet should be aligned.

Perfect posture
To give yourself the best possible chance of playing the shot you want, you'll need to get in the right position beforehand.

Eyes
Keep your eyes focused on the back of the ball throughout the shot.

Knees
Flex your knees a little for support as your body turns into the swing.

Waist
Make a slight bend at your waist, taking care not to go too low as this will cause you to raise your body up during the swing, making a good contact less likely.

WATCH IT
see DVD chapter 1

tips for better posture

The golf swing is an incredibly dynamic – if unnatural – movement. With so many moving parts, it's not surprising that things can go wrong. Achieving the right posture can dramatically reduce the mistakes in your game. And while your physical size and shape can affect your posture and the way in which you swing a club, the fundamental elements of the correct body position still apply to virtually every aspect of the game.

Driving
Make sure that you keep your chin high off your chest so you give yourself sufficient room for a full shoulder turn.

Iron play
Keep your shoulders back and your arms close to your body throughout the swing. You should never feel as if you're reaching for the ball.

Pitching
Bend from your waist and add extra flex to your knees. Your head should be almost over the ball.

Putting
When putting, you need to keep your head directly over the ball, so you have to bend from the waist. This creates a smooth pendulum effect as it lets the putter follow the movement of the shoulders and remain square to the line.

WATCH IT
see DVD chapter 1

stance

Your stance is the part of the set-up that provides a solid base from which you can successfully swing your club. The width of your stance depends upon which club you're using. When you're using the driver, because it's the longest club your feet will be wider apart than for any other club. If you're hitting with the shorter pitching wedge, you should adopt a narrow stance. It's important to remember that if your feet are too far apart you will not be able to achieve a full turn with your hips and shoulders – check by adopting your stance and seeing if your knees can reach each other. If they can't, you'll need to adjust your stance.

a Driving stance
When you're using the driver, your stance should be at its widest. As the club is the longest one you will use, you'll also need to stand back from the ball, which should be in a line with your left heel.

b Iron stance
The ideal stance when you're using irons should be with your feet positioned shoulder-width apart. The ball should be slightly forward of centre.

c Short-iron stance
The shorter your club, the narrower your stance should be – this helps to steepen the angle of the swing and create the loft needed to get the ball airborne quickly.

d Putting stance
When you're putting, adopt a wider stance. This gives you a solid foundation from which to make your shot. Keep your feet flat on the grass throughout the putt.

WATCH IT
see DVD chapter 1

The legendary American golfer Ben Hogan once wrote, "good golf begins with a good grip." He's right. Without the correct grip, you won't be able to control the clubface and your game will suffer. There are three main grips to choose from: the ten-finger, Vardon, and interlocking grips. Experiment with them to discover which one feels right for you.

getting a grip

Tips for a good grip

• Don't grasp the club too tightly as this can lead to tension in your arms and therefore your swing.

• You should feel the weight of the club more in your fingers than in your palms.

• Ignore the markings on the club grip – they're not meant to act as a guide for the position of your hands.

• A good grip should make hingeing your wrists much easier on the backswing.

a Ten-finger (baseball) grip
The simplest grip to master, the ten-finger grip is especially good for anybody with smaller hands. Start with a "lead hand" grip (if you're right-handed, your lead hand will be your left) with your thumb pointing down the shaft and the club's grip anchored under the heel pad of your hand. Place the little finger of your trailing hand close against the index finger of your lead hand. Cover your lead hand thumb with the lifeline of your trailing hand.

b Vardon (overlapping) grip
Named after Harry Vardon, who popularized the style at the turn of the 20th century, the Vardon grip is the most commonly used grip in golf. Take the little finger on your trailing hand and place it in the hollow between the middle and index finger on your lead hand. The thumb on your lead hand should slip in to your lifeline on your other hand.

c Interlocking grip
As used by Jack Nicklaus and Tiger Woods, the interlocking grip is the most popular among professionals. Take the little finger on your trailing hand and lace it with the index finger on your lead hand. Once again, the thumb on your lead hand should then fit into the lifeline of your trailing hand.

WATCH IT
see DVD chapter 1

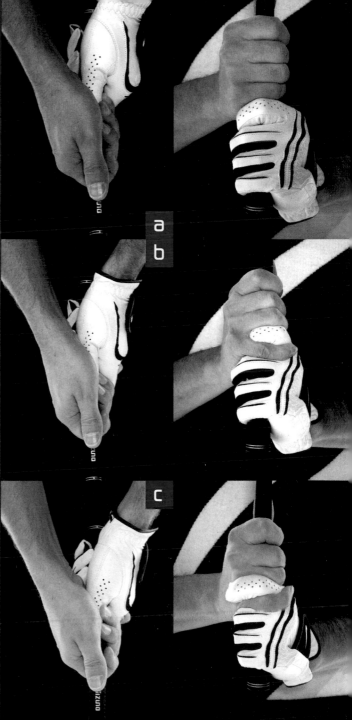

aim and alignment

Often, aim and alignment are mistakenly interpreted as the same thing, when the truth is that they're quite different.

Your aim refers to the direction in which the clubface points in relation to the target line, while alignment is the term given to the position of the body in relation to the target. Getting both elements right is crucial. If your clubface isn't square on impact or your body isn't in the right position before you swing, your chances of hitting the ball where you want it to go will be very slim.

a Open face
If you're right-handed, an open clubface will point to the right of the target line.

b Square face
If your clubface is square to the ball, then you will be aiming directly at the target.

c Closed face
When the clubface is in a closed position, your aim will be to the left of the target.

Alignment exercise

To help with alignment, place two clubs on the ground in parallel (see above). Imagine they are like a railway track – stand beneath the lower rail with the ball below the upper rail. Swing through, aiming to avoid the upper club, and the ball should sail away on the correct line.

WATCH IT
see DVD chapter 1

Get swinging
Head to the practice range and keep working on your swing until the movement feels natural.

Shoulder
On your backswing, your left shoulder should turn through 90° and rest under your chin.

Torso
As your shoulders turn, so too should your torso. Keep your eyes focused on the ball.

Knees
Flexed knees provide much-needed stability during the swing. You should also feel some resistance in your right thigh and right knee as you complete your backswing.

rhythm and motion

To maintain a great golf swing, you'll need to have rhythm and balance. When you watch professional golfers, you will notice how effortless they make the golf swing look. This is because they have a consistent tempo to their action and over their careers have developed a rhythm that is almost second nature to them. So if you want consistency and control, focus on improving your movement.

1 As you power through the ball, the speed of the club should pull your arms straight and then into the follow-through.

2 After contact, the right side of your body pushes through and your weight moves almost entirely onto your left side.

3 When you complete your swing, your chest should be pointing towards your target and your knees should always be together.

WATCH IT
see DVD chapter 2

building your swing

When you start playing golf it's very easy to become immersed in the technical aspects of the swing. Try not to. While an understanding of the mechanics of the swing sequence is useful, to begin with it's better to have lessons on a practice range and hit some balls with a professional looking on and advising.

Key points

• Building your golf swing is an ongoing process, requiring a lot of practice and considerable patience.

• Always take time to visualize the kind of shot that you want to play and then set up to give yourself the best chance of achieving it.

• Only start your swing when you are happy that your posture, aim, and alignment are all correct.

• The more you play and practice, the more your muscles will remember the mechanics of the golf swing. So after a while, your swing will become second nature.

1 First, begin with the address. Assume the correct stance and posture, then bring the club head to the ball.

4 The downswing describes the top of the backswing to the point of impact with the ball. The correct sequence on the downswing is: shift weight, rotate hips, and release your hands and arms.

2 The takeaway is the initial part of the backswing – bring the club back, parallel to the ground, through the movement of your shoulders. Keep your hands and arms in the same relative positions as at address.

3 Your wrists should be cocked only at the top of the backswing. Keep your club parallel to the ground, pointing directly at the target. Your weight should be transferred almost entirely to your right leg.

5 The follow-through is the final part of the swing during and after impact. The previous stages of the swing create the power; the follow-through helps to direct the ball.

6 Don't try to hit the ball too hard. While the speed of the swing will play a huge part in determining how far your shot goes, a solid contact at impact will still yield impressive results, even at a slower swing speed.

WATCH IT
see DVD chapter 2

head posture

Never underestimate the importance of your head position throughout the swing sequence. By keeping your head steady and your chin off your chest, you will give yourself the best chance of maximizing your power and in doing so, increase the distance you'll hit the ball. Don't look up before your follow-through, as this will seriously undermine your chances of achieving the desired result.

Posture checklist

• When you set up, try to think of your head as an extension of your spine.

• To create the right angle, imagine that you are about to dive into a swimming pool.

• As you address the ball, take time to look at the line from your ball to where you want to hit it. This will aid your alignment.

• Think about how you focus on the ball during the swing. Remember that your eyes should remain fixed on the back of the ball through the strike itself.

1 At address, your chin should be clear of your chest. As you begin your swing, let your head to move very slightly to the right to allow for a full shoulder turn.

2 Keep your head still throughout the downswing and remain focused on the ball through impact.

3 Raise your head on the follow-through. When you have completed your swing, you should be facing the target.

balance and weight transfer

There's a lot to remember about the swing, but the more you play, the more natural the process will become. Power and distance come from the coiling motion of the upper body and the correct transferral of weight, not sheer force. That's why it's crucial not to hit the ball too hard – you're trying to sweep the ball away with the club, not knock the casing off it. The best golfers have a smooth, consistent swing that looks almost effortless. Make this your goal.

1 Begin your swing by taking the club slowly away from the ball, with your front arm sliding across your chest. As you do this, transfer your weight to your rear foot.

2 At the top of your backswing, maintain the weight distribution put in place during your set-up. As you move towards the ball, transfer your weight to your front foot, so you move through the strike to a controlled finish.

3 Keep your head down throughout the impact, and extend your arms fully. As you turn with the swing and you transfer your weight fully to your front foot, your rear heel lifts to keep you balanced through the turn.

Balancing act
Everyone wants to hit the ball a long way, but you'll only achieve this through balanced movement.

Head
At the culmination of your swing you should be looking directly at the target.

Hands
Your hands should finish above your left shoulder, if you're right-handed, or your right shoulder, if if you're left-handed.

Hips
Your hips should rotate fully and end up facing the target squarely.

Feet
Your weight is now fully on your front foot, while balance is maintained by your rear foot.

WATCH IT
see DVD chapter 2 >

Distance control is a key element in playing successful golf, and knowing just how far you can hit the ball with each club in your bag will give you the confidence to play a more aggressive game. The best way to gauge this is by heading to the practice range. It's also a great idea to use the range before you play your round as it gets you swinging the club and loosening up before you make your way to the first tee.

on the practice range

- If you want to use the range, you'll need to pay for a basket of balls. You can get these from the machine that dispenses the balls – just remember to place your basket under it.

- If you mis-hit a shot and the ball only goes a short distance ahead of you, don't be tempted to retrieve it and hit it again as you may walk in front of another player and disrupt their game or, worse still, get hit by their ball.

Note your distance
Good golf is learned on the practice range, not on the course, so make a note of how far you're hitting those well-struck shots, then try to replicate it.

Shorter shots
If you need to work on your shorter shots, try using closer targets, such as the nets, to hone your skills. Take a sand wedge or a lob wedge and see if you can land the ball in the net.

Distance boards
Use the distance boards as targets and try to land your ball as close to them as you can. This will help you get a feel of how far you can hit the ball with a particular club.

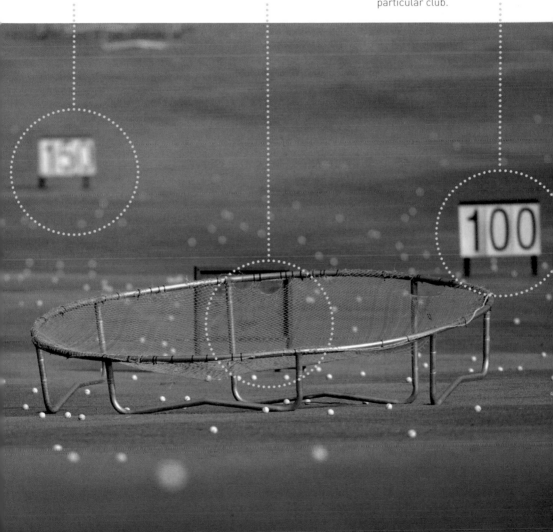

teeing up

a

b

c

d

Long iron
When you're using a long iron off the tee, you need only tee the ball up ever so slightly. Think of it as giving yourself the best lie that you can (see pages 82–83).

Short iron
If you're using a short iron, tee it up to a minimal level to give yourself the best possible chance of getting a clean contact and imparting some backspin on the ball.

Fairway wood
If you're using a fairway wood to tee off, then tee up the ball enough so that half of the ball is visible above the top of the club head. Do this and you'll stand a better chance of finding the sweet spot.

Driver
When you're teeing with a driver, be sure to tee the ball up with at least half of the ball visible above the clubface. This will help you to hit the ball on an upward path.

How high you tee the ball depends on which type of club you're going to use. The reason the height changes is due to the position of the "sweet spot" – the part of the clubface that produces optimum contact – which is different for each club. On a driver, for instance, the sweet spot is higher up the face, whereas it is lower on a 7-iron – so learn to tee it accordingly.

Recognize your tee
- When you reach the hole, you'll see three or four sets of colour-coded tee markers at varying distances from the green.

- Average players should play off the next set of markers, the yellow tees.

- Red tees are usually reserved for women players. These are placed nearest to the putting green.

WATCH IT
see DVD chapter 3

teeing off

For many players, the first tee is cause for intense anxiety – yet it shouldn't be. Try to remember that most players suffer the occasional bout of butterflies on the first tee, especially if there are people watching.

The secret of conquering your nerves is to think positively and pay attention to what you want to achieve on the hole, rather than to the other players looking at you. Try not to focus on the result of the shot you are about to play, but do focus on the actual process of hitting your ball. If you've set up correctly and made a good swing, your ball will find your chosen target.

Golden rules for teeing off

- Use a club that you know you can rely on. Take a few practice swings to loosen up, and then begin your pre-shot routine.

- Whatever you do, do not be hurried. While you want to get the shot away, it's good practice to take your time. Try breathing in and out through your nose. This can help get your heart rate down and ease your nerves.

- Don't hit the ball too hard – this only increases the likelihood of a poor result.

- A shorter tee shot that finds the fairway is nearly always preferable to a longer one that makes your next shot too difficult.

- If you've hit your ball into the rough, make a mental note of an object, say a tree or a bush, that it may have landed near. This will make the ball easier to find when you begin looking for it.

WATCH IT
see DVD chapter 3

driving

It's important to invest in the right club for your standard of play. You could spend a small fortune on a driver – and it can be tempting, when faced with the array of drivers available for every level – but if you are just starting out, it's never a wise investment. Before you buy, it's a good idea to seek advice from a qualified instructor on which club is right for your game, and as you progress, upgrade your clubs to match your higher standard of play.

Choose the appropriate club for the shot ahead of you. You may not always want to use a driver for a drive shot – for example, if the fairway is tight and space is at a premium, you may want to consider hitting an iron instead. It may cost you some distance, but it will help keep the ball out of trouble.

When you're taking a drive shot, you should also consider the necessary adjustment to your stance and tee height.

a A wide stance
When you're driving, you need to adopt a much wider stance than normal for added stability through the shot. If you're right handed, you should also drop your right shoulder a little lower than your left to help encourage a better shoulder turn.

b Tee it high
When you tee up your ball for a driver, it needs to be higher than it would be for any other club. This is because the "sweet spot" is located higher on the face than with irons.

approach shots

When you tee off on a par-four or par-five hole, you're aiming to put your ball in the safety of the fairway. On the fairway, the grass is shorter and more consistent, so you're almost guaranteed to benefit from a good lie from which to play your next shot.

If you've found the fairway, try to approach your ball by walking in line with your ball and the target. This will give you longer to survey your next shot and weigh up all your options. The secret to successful fairway or "approach" play is maintaining control. Never try to swing the club at full speed; not even professional players do that. Instead, shorten your backswing a little, and concentrate on accuracy.

Tips for fairway play

- Aim for the fairway, because landing a ball there eliminates the chance of a bad lie and gives you the best angle into the putting green.

- If you find the fairway, take full advantage. Don't be afraid to take a divot. After all, a good divot taken after impact is often the sign of a well-struck ball.

- When you reach your ball, take time to weigh up your next shot. What distance do you have left to the green? And how far is it to the flag itself? Check to see where the nearest distance marker is.

- A stroke saver distance guide is an invaluable reference for checking course yardages – most clubhouses have them for sale.

on the fairway

When you arrive at your ball and you've decided on the shot you want to play, go through your pre-shot routine. It's a good idea to start from behind the ball and choose your ideal target line (see above). Doing this will also help you envisage precisely the kind of shot – and outcome – you desire.

Make sure that you have the right club for the shot ahead and try to picture the flight of the ball as it leaves the clubface and heads towards the putting green. Visualizing the shot not only helps to eradicate any doubts you may have, but makes it feel great when you actually execute the shot just as you had imagined.

Good timing

If you're on the fairway and about to shoot for the green, first look out for players ahead of you. If there are people on the putting green ahead, you should always wait until they have completed the hole and left the putting surface before you play your shot.

Safe play

If you don't think that you can reach the green with your next shot, it's often a safer play to "lay up." This means playing a controlled shot that's deliberately aimed short of the putting green, rather than hitting the ball as hard as you can and hoping for the best.

A key component of effective approach play is what's called the "lie" of your ball, or how it sits on the ground after it has come to rest.

If you've found the fairway, then it's likely you'll have a good lie from which to plan your next shot. A good lie is important because it gives you options and allows you to consider a range of shots that a bad lie will not (such as a "tight lie", when the ball is sitting on dirt with very little grass beneath it). If your ball has landed in a good lie, you can be more aggressive with your shot, safe in the knowledge that nothing unexpected will happen as the ball leaves the clubface.

the lie of the ball

A good lie

When the ball is sitting up on a flat section of the fairway, with grass underneath, and free from any impediments around it, you have a good lie. This means you stand a much better chance of making a clean contact with the ball.

A bad lie

If you fail to find the fairway, your chances of making the green with your second shot may be seriously reduced, depending on the golf course. If you have a bad lie, such as being in the rough, think about what golf coaches call "risk versus reward". In other words, is it worth getting yourself in more trouble when there is a safer option?

perfect pitch

You'll need to employ the pitch shot when you're close to the green, but beyond the range for a chip shot (see pages 88–89). Your aim is to hit the ball high enough for it to land softly on the green and stop quickly.

When you're planning a pitch, visualize where you want the ball to land, then practise the length of swing you feel you'll need to execute the shot. Distance control is the key. Keeping your basic swing the same, use a longer backswing for longer pitches and a shorter one for shorter shots.

a Club
Concentrate on letting the pitching wedge's lofted clubface lift the ball into the air – don't try to scoop it up.

b Grip
Use your regular grip but with your hands marginally ahead of your ball at address.

c Stance
Your stance is narrow and the ball should be slightly back beyond the centre of your stance.

Golden rules

- When you're pitching, your follow-through should be the same length as your backswing (see left).

- Your weight at set-up should be slightly on your front foot. Keep your lower body stable throughout the swing.

- Control is crucial, so shorten your normal backswing.

- Strike down crisply into the back of the ball. A good contact should give increased spin, and will help the ball to stop more quickly.

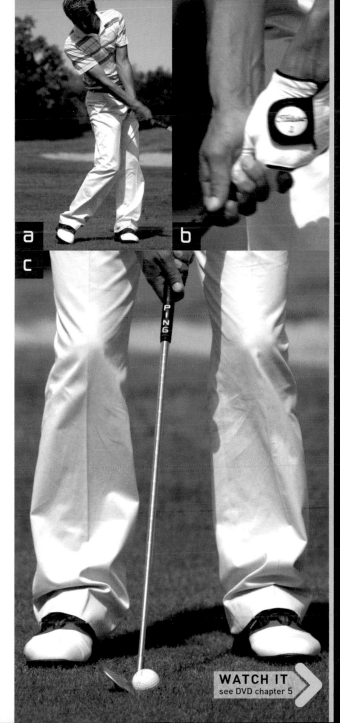

WATCH IT
see DVD chapter 5

The flop shot

Although risky, the flop shot – a high pitch – is great when you need to get the ball up and over an obstacle and onto the green. Take your sand wedge (or lob wedge, if you have one), put the ball slightly forward in your stance, open the clubface, and keep your hands level with the ball (see left, above).

Now, aim slightly left of the target, as you would if you were in a bunker. Take the club back on a steeper angle than normal and when you return the club face to the ball, make sure the club clips the grass as it slides under the ball (see left, below). Always try to make a longer follow-through than backswing and the result should be a shot that soars straight up and lands softly on the green.

pitching options

When you're pitching, first try to find out just how far you can hit a pitch shot by using different lengths of backswing, making a note of how far each shot goes. Then try some variations on the shot, such as the bump and run, in which you put the ball back in your stance and hit it lower, allowing the ball to run up on the green, or the flop shot, where the ball is hit so high that it stops on the green with very little roll. The more you experiment, the more idea you'll have of just what you can do with the pitch shot.

a Angle of attack
To execute the basic pitch shot, take your club back at a much steeper angle than for your normal swing.

b Get more spin
To get more spin on the ball and make it stop more quickly on the green, put the ball back in your stance and accelerate through the ball.

c Finish
After impact, your right arm and hand should release into the follow-through. As the ball leaves the clubface, your body should move towards the target. Only lift up your head when the ball is well on its way to the green.

WATCH IT
see DVD chapter 5

chipping basics

The ability to chip well can make all the difference between an average round and a great one. But when should you chip, and what club should you use?

You'll need to chip when your ball is near the green, but not on the actual putting surface itself. The object of the chip shot is to get the ball up in the air quickly so that it clears the longer grass surrounding the putting green – called the "apron" – and lands on the short, consistent grass of the green before rolling up to the hole. To play this shot effectively you should use a lofted club, such as a pitching wedge, that will propel the ball upwards.

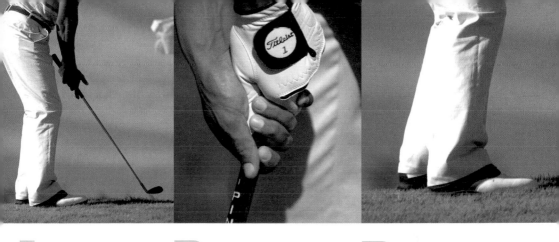

1 To set up for a chip shot, move your feet closer together than for a normal iron shot. The ball should be further back in your stance.

2 Grip the club lightly, but with firm wrists. Keep your hands ahead of the ball and the club shaft angled towards the hole for a clean strike.

3 Remember to place most of your weight on your front foot and keep it there throughout the shot.

4 When you focus on the strike, it's important that you commit to the shot and accelerate through the ball.

5 Keep your head, legs, and upper body still as you swing from the arms and shoulders, not the wrists.

6 Don't worry that the ball won't get airborne – play it correctly, and the clubface will propel the ball upwards.

WATCH IT see DVD chapter 5 ▶

effective chipping techniques

The chip is a key shot in any golfer's armoury. Not only is it one of the simpler shots to execute, it's invaluable for extricating you from any difficult situations you may find yourself in around the green. As long as you remember that the key to successful chipping is accelerating into the impact and letting the clubface lift the ball up and onto the putting surface, you'll keep your scores heading in the right direction.

Golden rules

• Gently lean your upper body towards the target.

• Keep your head steady and your eyes fixed on the ball until you have hit it.

• Keep the clubface square to the path of the swing throughout.

• Keep the club head close to the ground as it moves back and through.

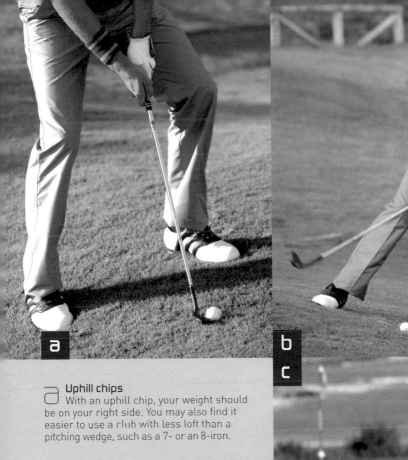

Uphill chips
With an uphill chip, your weight should be on your right side. You may also find it easier to use a club with less loft than a pitching wedge, such as a 7- or an 8-iron.

Downhill chips
The chip from a downhill lie requires your weight to be on your leading side. Be careful not to decelerate through impact, as you may stub the club head into the ground instead of following through correctly.

Bump and run
The bump and run can be used when you have a long chip shot ahead of you. By using a club with a less lofted face than a pitching wedge, an 8-iron, for example, you can lower the trajectory of the ball and allow it to land sooner and run up to the hole rather than fly through the air.

putting

Professional golfers have a saying – "Drive for show, putt for dough".
Why do they say it? Because of all the shots in the game of golf, putting is
the one discipline that can render worthless all the good work you have
put in getting from tee to green. If you're going to shoot low scores, you'll
need to putt well. Here's how.

1 Adopt a stance with the ball nearer to your front foot and the putter face square to your target line. Hold the putter lightly, but try to keep your wrists firm. Allow your arms to hang down like a pendulum.

2 Take a few practice swings to gauge the speed at which you'll need to hit the ball. Now take the putter back smoothly, swinging from your shoulders.

3 From the top of your backswing, bring the putter head down smoothly so that it arrives square to the target on impact. Hit "through" the ball, keeping your wrists firm and your head still.

Key points

• Always keep your head still and your eyes over the ball when you're putting.

• Keep your legs stable through the stroke, and maintain a slight flex in the knees.

• Watch the putter connect with the back of the ball. If you've hit it correctly, it should feel as though your rear hand is guiding the ball to the hole.

• Like pitching, your follow-through should be the same length as your backswing.

• Practise your putting by keeping your head perfectly still, even after impact. Then listen for the sound of the ball dropping into the hole. This will help you to develop a smooth, reliable putting stroke.

WATCH IT
see DVD chapter 6

tips for better putting

Putting is what's called a "feel" shot. It's a discipline that requires skill and judgment, co-ordination and finesse. The putter is the most used club in the golf bag – you may use your driver 13 or 14 times during a round, whereas you'll take out your putter at least twice as often on a good day, and more on a very bad one. That's why putting practice is vital. So next time you work on your game, put the driver down and head off to the practice green – it could save you a whole lot of strokes.

a Choose your line
Try to envisage how the ball will get to the hole, accounting for any undulations in the putting surface. This is called "reading the green". Don't worry if you can't pick the right line straight away – it will get easier the more you play.

b Double-check
Take a look at your putt from different angles. Crouching down is a good idea as it gives you a better perspective on the slope of the green.

c Hold on
Putting grips are a very individual issue, and can differ enormously from one player to the next. Find the one that you feel comfortable with. Remember, any grip that yields consistent results is a good grip.

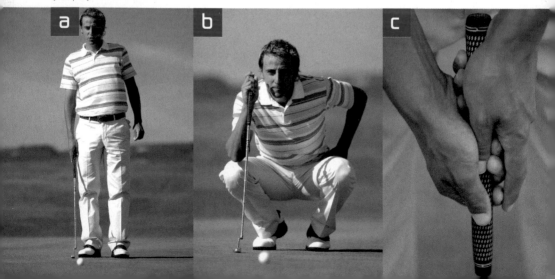

Get it right
Adopting the right position is crucial for good putting. Use this drill to check that you're setting up correctly.

Head position
Your eyes should be directly over your ball when you are putting. Try dropping another ball from your nose onto a ball below to check that you're in the right position.

Direct hit
If you've assumed the correct position then the two balls should hit each other. If they don't, adjust your position and try again.

WATCH IT >
see DVD chapter 6

putting practice

Practising your putting is one of the best ways to lower your scores. Not only will it help you to develop a better putting stroke, but it will also improve your judgment of speed and distance and, in doing so, increase your confidence when you are on the putting green.

The further you are from the hole the less likely you are to hole a putt, so the secret is to make sure that if you miss you leave the ball close enough to the hole to make the next putt a formality. Here's a couple of drills designed to help you hole out.

Long putts
When you're practising those longer putts, try this exercise (see above). Take a handful of tees and place them in a semi-circle around the back of the hole – a radius of 0.4 m (18 in) to 0.6 m (2 ft) should be enough. Now take five balls and try to ensure that each of the putts stays within the semi-circle. If you fail, then repeat the exercise until you succeed. As you improve, lengthen the distance of the putts.

Short putts

Even professional players sometimes miss the short putts. If you want to master the art of holing those tricky little shots, try this simple round the clock exercise. Place 12 balls in a circle around the hole to create a "clock face", and then try to hole each of them in succession. If you miss one ball, start again from the beginning. As you improve, increase the distance between the balls, so widening the circle.

WATCH IT
see DVD chapter 6

reading the green

Developing a smooth, reliable putting stroke is just the first step in becoming a consistent putter. To progress from good putter to great putter you must master the speed, and what's called the "break", of your putt. This means judging the contours of the green and knowing how hard you'll need to hit the ball.

Reading greens begins with understanding how your ball reacts when rolling up, down, or across a slope. If it's an uphill putt you'll need to hit your ball harder than on a level green. If it's downhill, don't strike the ball so hard. When putting across a slope, aim wide of the target and try to determine how much the ball will curve on its way to the hole.

a On the green
Before you start your round, spend a little time on the practice green. This will help you gauge the speed of the greens on the course.

b Short cuts
Don't be tentative when taking short putts. It's often easier to hole them when you hit them firmly and take any break out of the putt.

c Watch and learn
Before you take your shot, examine the break from a variety of angles and make a mental note of how any of your playing partner's putts react on the way to green.

d Be positive
When you've picked your line and gauged the speed, be positive and trust your putting stroke. The worst mistake in putting is leaving the putt short, so hit it hard enough to ensure that it stops just before the hole.

fault fixing: hooks and slices

While the object for all beginners is to hit the ball straight, it's often easier said than done. The trouble is there are so many component parts of the swing that when one goes wrong it can easily lead to other mistakes – so that the ball never seems to go where you want it to.

The hook
The hook is when the ball deviates from the target line and curves to the left. Here's what you need to consider to avoid hooking the ball.

• When you address the ball, ensure that your clubface is square to the ball when you set up. If it's not, then you stand little chance of it being square on impact.

• Your grip may be too strong. Turn your hands anti-clockwise and ensure that the same number of knuckles is visible on both hands when you look down.

The slice
Slicing the ball occurs when the ball curves from left to right (for right-handed players) and it's caused by any number of basic faults in your set up and swing. Consider the following points:

• Check that you're lining up with the right target. Your stance should be square to the target.

• Align your shoulders, hips, and feet square to the target, or you'll be swinging from "out to in" and exercising sidespin on the ball, the very thing that produces the slice.

• Your grip may be weak. Turn your hands anti-clockwise – you should see the same number of knuckles on both hands when you look down.

fault fixing: the swing

Ask any golfer what the best feeling in golf is, and they'll tell you that it has to be the moment when they have played a shot exactly the way they had planned, and finished with the result that they had hoped for.

Of course, that doesn't always happen, and this can be attributed to a variety of causes. By working on the flaws in your swing you can significantly increase your chances of playing your perfect golf shot and putting the ball where you intend. But be warned – practice can become as addictive as playing a round!

a Slow and smooth
Trying to hit the ball too hard can often lose you distance and accuracy. Although it may cost a few yards on the fairway, you may want to shorten your backswing and keep control.

b Get set
It's important to have good posture and balance to execute a good swing. Don't reach for the ball – keep your spine straight and bend from the waist. You'll need to stand taller when using a wood.

c Take it away
You need plenty of width in your backswing if you want to maximize your distances. So take the club away low to the ground, and don't hinge your wrists too early.

d Back and through
On the downswing, your right elbow should descend towards your right hip. You'll need to keep your wrists hinged until late into the approach to the ball.

a b c

fault fixing: common problems

Part of the fun and frustration of playing golf is finding the flaws in your game and smoothing them out. Whereas one day you may leave the course cursing your luck or your swing, or both, there will be other days when those little changes you have made to your game finally pay dividends.

If improvement is slow in coming, don't be hard on yourself; no one in history has ever played the perfect round of golf. Keep experimenting, keep practising, stay positive, and you'll fix your faults and improve your scores.

Swing for a pitch
Never forget that the swing for a pitch shot doesn't differ markedly from your normal swing. So remember to keep your front arm straight on the backswing. Also try to maintain the flex in your knees and bend forward from the hips as you set up.

Visualize the chip shot
If you find that your greenside chips are falling short or racing through the green, picture the shot by imagining how you would throw the ball if you wanted to get it as close to the hole as possible. This will give you a better idea of where you should be looking to land the ball.

Bunkered!
The key to getting your bunker shots close to the hole is in your set-up. Remember to align yourself to the left of the target, if you're right handed, or to the right, if you're left handed, and maintain most of your weight on your leading side. Notice how open the greenside bunker shot stance should be.

Putting things right
One of the most common putting problems that beginners encounter is deceleration on their stroke. The way to eradicate this flaw is to work on the ideal pendulum motion. Place a club under your arms and across your chest, parallel with your target line. Now try some putts, making sure you don't allow the club to drop to the ground. This will help you to form good habits.

go play a round

coming up...

Golf etiquette: 110–113

Courtesy and etiquette on the golf course are considered important parts of the game. Find out what is expected of you and what you can do to make your round an even more enjoyable experience.

Playing awkward lies: 114–117

Uphill, downhill, sidehill – different lies require different techniques. Discover how to play them with confidence and style.

Playing Bunkers: 118-127

Once you understand how to escape from them successfully, bunkers and others hazards will hold no fear. Here are solutions to common problems, plus ways to get out of that bunker mentality that can undermine an otherwise good round.

Reaching the putting green: 128–131

The do's and don'ts of the putting green, from tending the flag to marking your ball.

courtesy on the golf course

Golf etiquette means showing courtesy and consideration while you're on the course. Keeping quiet while fellow golfers play or refraining from playing your shot until those ahead are out of distance is, naturally, common sense, but if you're in any doubt about what you should be doing and when you should be doing it, always ask for guidance.

Golden rules of golf etiquette

- When you reach the putting green, don't forget the shots your playing partners may have. Be careful not to walk on the line of anyone else's putt, and when you remove the flag from the hole, place it on an area of the green away from the hole that won't be involved in play.

- When you've finished playing a hole, and have replaced the flag, don't wait around next to the green totting up your score. Proceed straight to the next tee and do it there instead.

- Slow play is the bane of most golfers' lives. It is frustrating, irritating and, usually, unnecessary. So maintain a good pace to your round and try not to delay. Spend no longer than five minutes looking for a lost ball – any longer, and you'll not only be breaking the rules but you'll incur the wrath of the players behind you.

- If you're playing in a three ball or four ball (see golf talk, pages 152–55) you're obliged to allow any two-player groups to "play through". This means letting them go ahead of you.

pitch marks and divots

There's nothing more irritating than finding a green that is riddled with pitch marks or hitting a great drive down the middle of the fairway only to find that your ball has landed in a divot hole. Some rounds you'll find that

1 Repairing a pitch mark
When the greens are soft, it's inevitable that your ball will leave a mark on the putting surface.

2 Always use a pitch mark repairer or a tee. Never try to flatten the mark with a club or your shoe.

1 Replacing a Divot
It's a common misconception among beginners that taking a divot when you hit the ball is a bad thing. It's not.

2 A correctly played approach shot will often produce a divot, so don't be afraid to take one – just remember to replace it.

you cause damage almost every time you play a shot. Be considerate to other players by taking time to repair your pitch marks and divots properly.

WATCH IT
see DVD chapter 5

3 Insert your pitch mark tool to the back of the ball mark and pull the turf up and towards the centre of the damage, before repeating the action on all sides of the mark.

4 When you've made your way around the pitch mark, gently tap your putter over the affected area, flattening the surface. If you have time, repair any other pitch marks you may see as well.

3 When you make a divot, simply walk up to where the tuft of grass has landed and pick it up, before returning to where you hit your shot.

4 Place it in the exact spot it came from and then step on the grass you've replaced until the playing surface is smooth once more.

uphill and downhill lies

On some occasions, your ball won't always find a level area of grass. What you need to remember is that on uneven lies your swing will remain the same but you will need to change your set-up and your choice of club. On uphill and downhill lies, try to work with the slope rather than against it, replicating a level lie by setting up your body perpendicular to the slope.

a

b

a Uphill lie

When you're faced with an uphill lie, your ball will fly higher than usual. Work with this by taking one more club than normal. So if you would usually take a 7-iron, take a 6-iron instead. Set the ball further forward in your stance than usual, and when you take the club back, keep your back leg firm. During your downswing, transfer the weight to your front leg and finish your swing with the all-important shoulder turn.

b Downhill lie

For a downhill lie, work in reverse to the uphill lie. Choose one less club than normal, as the ball will fly lower (and therefore travel further) and position the ball back in your stance. When you play the shot, your weight should be on your front foot, and as you swing you should feel your hands following the line of the hill. If the slope is particularly steep, you may also need to hinge your wrists more, to avoid hitting the ground on your backswing.

WATCH IT
see DVD chapter 4

playing from a slope

One of the most difficult shots to play is when the ball comes to rest on the side of a hill. However, if you manage to maintain your balance throughout the stroke and adjust your set-up to allow for the incline, you'll soon discover that there's not too much to be worried about.

When the ball is below your feet, you should sit back on your heels as you prepare to make your shot. There will be a tendency to slice the ball since your swing plane is more upright, but you can allow for this by aiming more to the left than usual. Grip your club as near to the end as possible so that you can use its full length, then flex your knees and tilt your upper body downwards.

Set up to succeed

Don't be fazed by a hilly lie. Adapt your set-up and approach the shot with confidence, and you'll find it much easier to play.

Hands

When the ball is above your feet, you'll be nearer to it than you would be on level ground, so grip lower down the handle of your club.

Aim

There will be a tendency to hook the ball to the left so adjust your set-up and aim slightly to the right of the target.

Stance

Keep your weight on your toes throughout the shot.

WATCH IT
see DVD chapter 4

in the bunker

For so many beginners, escaping from a bunker is the stuff of nightmares. Just the thought conjures up images of shot after shot spent hacking away in the sand, all to no avail. Yet the truth is that when you know what to do, there really isn't very much to be afraid of. Whether you're splashing your way out of a greenside bunker or escaping a fairway trap, if you have the right techniques you will soon discover that getting your ball out of the sand can be one of the simpler shots you'll play.

Escaping sand traps

- Adjusting your set-up is key. Dig your feet into the sand and get a more solid foundation for your shot.

- When playing out of a greenside bunker, aim just to the left of the target if you are right handed, and just to the right if you are left handed.

- For fairway bunker shots, try to hit the sand 2.5 cm (1 in) behind the ball.

- For all bunker shots, keep your eyes focused on the point at which you want the clubface to enter the sand.

- Whatever your position, remember to accelerate through the ball.

Choose the right club

Fairway bunkers are usually fairly shallow and allow you to make regular club selections according to the distance you need to make. For shots from greenside bunkers, which are often quite steep, you'll need to use a sand wedge. This is an iron that has a very lofted face (typically 56°) and is specially designed to bounce off the undersurface of a bunker. Its flat profile produces an explosion of sand that helps lift the ball out of bunker and onto the green.

Avoid penalties

Never ground your club in the sand before you play a bunker shot. If you do, you'll face a penalty.

WATCH IT
see DVD chapter 4

greenside bunkers

It may sound strange, but when playing the greenside bunker shot you should deliberately aim to miss the ball. This is because your target is an area of sand about 2.5 cm (an inch or so) behind the ball. Striking the surface of the bunker here creates a pocket of sand that helps to lift the ball up and forward, and out of the sand trap.

1 Get a solid base for your feet. Take your sand wedge and address the ball with the clubface open and your body aiming left of the flag (right if you are left handed). The ball should be in the middle of your stance. Adopt a firmer grip than usual, with your hands level with the ball. Bend your knees and move your weight to your front foot to encourage a steep swing.

2 Hover your club behind the ball and pick a mark in the bunker where you want the clubhead to enter the sand. This is your target. You should be looking to sweep away a section of sand about the size of a banknote when you play the shot. Keeping your head steady, take the club back more sharply than you would for a regular iron shot.

3 As you swing back towards the ball you should feel as if you're cutting across the ball, or, as golf coaches say, from outside to in. While this may feel unnatural, trust your swing. Even though you think you're going to hit the ball too far left, the fact that your clubface is open will actually take the ball to the right.

4 As ever, it's vital that you accelerate through the ball when you play your shot. Similarly, you should also make a proper follow-through with a good hip and shoulder turn. The last thing you want is the club stopping in the sand and the ball staying in the bunker.

fairway bunkers

Finding your ball in a fairway bunker presents an entirely different challenge to being caught in a greenside sand trap. You'll need to take a much longer shot, so you'll be using a different club. You won't be trying to achieve an explosive effect when splashing out of a bunker near the green – instead, you should aim to nip the ball off the top of the sand.

1 When you set up for a fairway-bunker shot you need a solid base to work from, so dig your feet into the sand and make sure the ball is slightly forward in your stance. This will help you to strike the ball on the up, reducing the chance of taking too much sand.

2 Now grip the club a little further down the handle, again with a slightly firmer hold. Try to keep the lower half of your body still throughout the stroke.

3 This shot isn't about raw power – it's about control – so take more club than you need and consider shortening your backswing.

4 In the fairway bunker, you'll be looking to nip the ball off the surface of the trap, taking as little sand as possible and maximizing the shot's distance.

5 Accelerate through the ball, complete a full follow-through and you should see your ball heading towards the green.

in the rough

While escaping from bunkers is all about exercising control, escaping from thick rough is one of the few situations on the golf course in which you'll need to use raw power. To get your ball out of the rough and back in play, think carefully before taking decisive action and adjust your stance before you take the shot.

a Think first
The first thing to do is assess the situation and decide upon the best course of action. Don't be greedy. If the green is a long way away and your ball is barely visible in the rough, you should reconsider going for the green.

b Keep wrists firm
Next, make sure that your wrists are firm throughout the strike. This is vital because as the club moves through the rough, the grass will tug at it, and may pull it off line.

c Shift your weight
Grip down the club slightly and set the ball back in your stance. As you're going to need your body weight to help power the ball out, shift your weight to your leading leg. This will help increase club head speed through the ball.

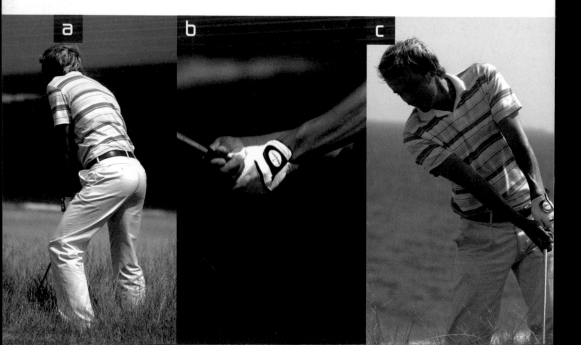

Rough play

Confidence and commitment to your shot will help you play successfully from the rough.

Focus

Even though you're hitting the ball harder, try to keep focused on the ball throughout the shot.

Hands

Keeping your wrists firm ensures that the clubface is as square to the ball as possible on contact.

Legs

Move your weight to your leading leg as you move through your downswing. This helps to maximize power.

WATCH IT
see DVD chapter 4

more hazards

Hazards can wreck a good round of golf. Whether your hazard is a pond or a bush, you need to be aware of the options available to you, and then make an informed decision about whether to play your ball.

Ask yourself if you can get the ball back in play or whether the chance of getting even further into trouble is simply too much to risk. For instance, if you find your ball in a hedge and there's no way you can get a club to it, it's best all round to declare it "unplayable" and accept a penalty shot. If you take this option, you'll then be entitled to drop the ball within two club-lengths of where it came to rest, but no closer to the hole. If you're in any doubt about what you can and can't do when your ball lands in a hazard, consult someone who knows.

a In the water
If your ball lands in casual water, such as a puddle on the fairway, you are entitled to drop it on dry ground without penalty. But if your ball lands in a water hazard (marked by yellow stakes) it will cost you a penalty stroke unless you decide to play the ball as it lies. In most cases you won't be able to get your ball out of the water, so it is usually best to play what is known as the percentage, or safer, shot.

b Dropping the ball
When you need to drop the ball, hold it in your hand with your arm outstretched at shoulder height and release it straight down to the ground.

c Options for an unplayable ball
If you've declared your ball unplayable, you have several options. The most common is to drop the ball within two club-lengths of where it came to rest. Mark the ball's position with a tee, then pick it up. Next, take your longest club and measure two club-lengths in the direction of the nearest point of relief (but no closer to the hole). Mark this spot with another tee. You should then drop your ball within these two marks. You can also go back to the place where you played the previous shot and take another. In both cases you will have to take a one-shot penalty.

on the green

When you reach the putting green you shouldn't just be concerned with holing out. There are a number of key matters to consider, from repairing the green to marking and cleaning your ball. When you are playing with other people, it is on the putting green that courtesy and etiquette are most important.

Guidelines on the green

- When your ball is on the green you may clean it. First, stand behind the ball, in a line with the flag, and place a marker behind it to mark its position.

- Repair any marks made by golf balls you see on the green. Damage caused by golf-shoe spikes can only be repaired once you've completed the hole.

- Always allow the player whose ball is furthest from the hole to play first.

- If your playing partner is a long way from the hole, offer to tend the flag. This gives them a better idea of the location of the hole.

- When removing the flag, place it on the edge of the green or on an area of the putting surface that is away from the hole and not involved in play.

- When you're considering a putt, be careful not to walk across the lines of other players' putts.

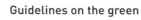

go further

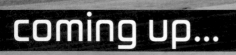

Loosening up: 134–135

Before you take to the first tee, it's vital to warm up your muscles. Protect against potential injury and improve your agility by stretching your trunk, shoulders, and back.

Refining your performance 136–139

If you're going to be good at golf, you'll need to master the art of risk and course management. Learn how to choose the right shot for any given situation.

Tournaments: 140–143

Major golf tournaments take place throughout the year. Find out why watching the professionals at work is a great way to learn and pick up tips.

Golf and travel: 144–149

There's a whole world of golf out there just waiting to be discovered. Investigate great locations for golfing holidays.

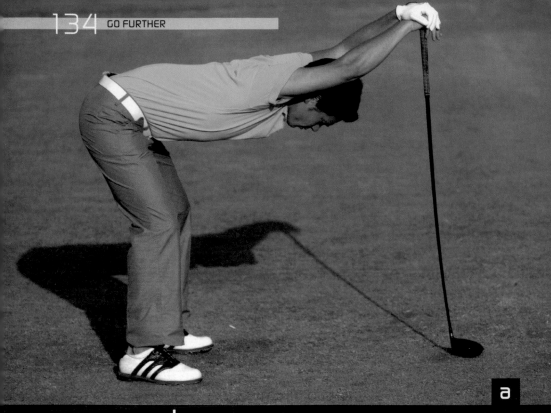

a

pre-round warm-ups

Playing golf to a good standard requires a certain amount of physical fitness and conditioning. Increasingly, the world's best players are devoting more time to training, and you too should try to keep in shape to improve your stamina levels and enhance your flexibility and power.

Before you hit that first tee shot, make sure you warm up by stretching your back, trunk, and shoulders. Not only will this help you swing more freely, but doing so will reduce your chances of injury. However, don't overdo the stretching – stretch gently at first to gradually warm your muscles and avoid muscle strain, and hold the stationary poses for no longer than five seconds.

a Back stretch
Place your driver in front of you, with your hands on the top of the grip and your arms outstretched, and push until you feel your back muscles stretching.

b Shoulder-blade stretch
Take one of your irons and hold it above your head in one hand. Bring your other hand round to hold the club handle and extend your upper arm until you feel the tension.

c Back rotation
Grip both ends of your driver and place it across your shoulder blades. With your feet flat on the ground, slowly rotate your upper body, replicating the motion your body follows when you swing the golf club.

d Trunk stretch
Hold the club head of an iron in your left hand and the grip in your right hand. Now reach as high as you comfortably can and bend your torso towards the ground. Hold the pose for five seconds, and then repeat on the other side.

e Shoulder stretch
Bring one arm across your chest and use your other arm to pull it towards you. You should feel the back of your shoulder stretching. Hold the position for five seconds and repeat with your other arm.

risk management

While making mistakes is all part of the game, it's always worth weighing up all your options. Is there anything to be gained by playing what appears to be a risky shot?

Tiger Woods may be able to hit his drive into the trees and still salvage the situation, but you may want to consider less ambitious options and instead focus on minimizing the effect of any mistakes you do make.

Risk tactics

• Once you've decided on your shot, it's important that you have the courage of your convictions and commit to it. A half-hearted attempt will often land you in even more trouble.

• Think about strategy when you're playing a round. Choosing the right club at the right time will help keep your score down.

• Going for position and not power will nearly always yield a better result.

• If your ball finds trouble in the rough or the trees, don't panic. Try to find the safest route back to the fairway.

Be cool
Being over-confident can cost you dearly on the golf course. Always pause and use your judgment to determine the best potential shot, and if that means you must take a penalty, then so be it.

Learn from other players
Whenever possible, observe your fellow players to see if there is anything that you can learn from their shot. Did they hit too far or too short? And what club did they use?

Attend to the small putt
If you've chipped up to the hole and left yourself with a small putt, don't be tempted to step up and knock it in. Give it the same consideration as other putts, and make sure that you hole it.

Keep thinking
Practising your swing on the tee will help you to visualize the shot ahead of you, and will also give you time to re-assess the potential danger ahead.

course management

Playing the right shots at the right time is known as "course management". Knowing when to attack and when to play a safe shot comes with experience, but the more you play the more you'll recognize the dangers on each hole.

The best course of action is to play to your strengths. So if you tend to slice the ball to the right with your driver, and there is an out-of-bounds area to the right side of the fairway, use a club you can rely on to hit straight and play away from hazards or the rough. You may lose distance, but your ball will stay in play.

Golden rules of course management

- When you reach the tee, take a moment to familiarize yourself with the hole ahead of you and weigh up where you want to put the ball for your next shot. If you're new to the course, look at the map of the hole on your score card and plan your strategy accordingly.

- Ask yourself if you can hit the ball far enough to take any bunkers out of play. Do you have enough loft on your club to clear any trees? How strong is the wind? Ascertain wind direction by throwing a handful of grass in the air.

- If you tend to slice or hook the ball, never aim at the hazard or rough in the hope that your ball will curve away from it. Think positively, and aim away.

- When you're hitting a tee shot, tee the ball up on the same side as any hazard or the rough. Psychologically, you'll get the feeling that you are aiming away from the trouble spot.

watching the professionals

If you visit a professional golf tournament you'll soon realize just how good the professional players are. But while it may have taken them years to reach the top of their game, you can learn a lot by watching them play. So if you're keen to improve your game, study the professionals as they go about their round. Note the fluid way they swing the club and the way they make the game look so effortless. Take note, too, of how they read their putts and play bunker shots. Then take what you've observed to the practice range.

a

b

c

a **Michelle Wie**
Having turned professional at the age of 16, Michelle Wie is tipped to become a golfing great.

b **Tiger Woods**
Arguably the greatest player to have picked up a golf club, Woods has taken the game to an entirely new level.

c **Sergio Garcia**
Nicknamed "El Niño", Spain's Sergio Garcia is one of a band of swashbuckling young players that have helped transform the image of golf.

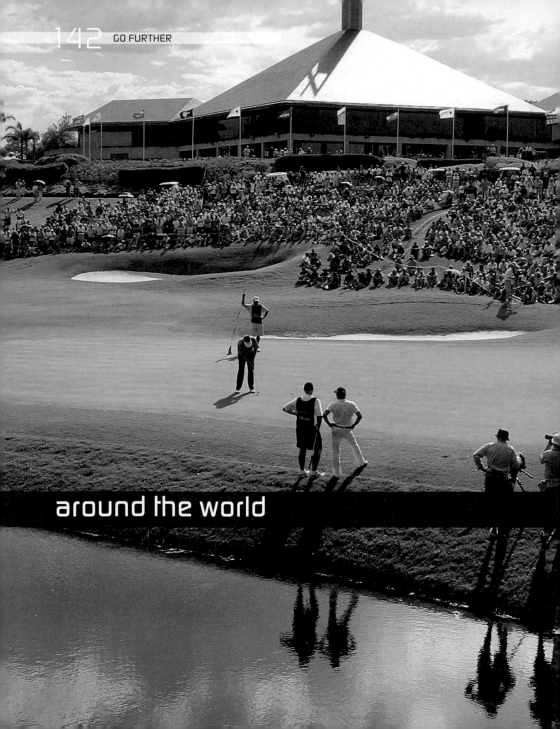

around the world

There are hundreds of golf tournaments held around the world each year, from Australia (see left) to Alaska. Those with the highest profiles are the four major championships. However, these are matched for excitement and competetiveness by a few key representative cup matches.

Golf's Top Tournaments

• Held in April, the Masters is the first major of the year. It differs from the other majors in that it is always played on the same golf course, the Augusta National in Augusta, Georgia, USA.

• The US Open was first played in 1895 and is known as the toughest of all of the majors. It takes place each June.

• The Open Championship, held in Britain in July, is the oldest of all the four majors, dating back to 1860.

• The US PGA Championship, played each August, is the year's final major.

• The Ryder Cup, held biennially, is played between the USA and Europe. It began in 1927 and has become one of the biggest events in the sporting calendar.

• Women's golf also has four majors: the Kraft Nabisco Championship in April, the LPGA (Ladies Professional Golf Association) Championship in June, the US Women's Open Championship in July, and the Women's British Open Championship, in August.

getting out there

The game of golf is now played on every continent, and there are many different types of course in a wide variety of settings. From the famous links courses of Scotland and Ireland to the desert courses springing up in Australia and the Middle East, each course offers its own unique challenge. The test for you, the golfer, is to take what you've learned so far and using your imagination and judgment, negotiate your way round, wherever you may be.

golf holidays

When you take up the game you will soon discover that there is a whole world of golf just waiting to be explored. Taking a golf holiday is a great way to combine playing your favourite sport with visiting some of the most beautiful areas of the world. From quick weekend breaks to resort-based package deals with tuition included, there is a huge variety of golf holidays to be enjoyed.

Top Golf-holiday Destinations

• Portugal

Head to the Algarve where the weather is perfect all year round, and where there are dozens of quality golf courses to choose from, including the famous Penina and Quinta do Lago.

• Florida

There are over 1,000 golf courses in the state of Florida, catering for every standard of player. With year-round sunshine and some of the best resorts in the world, Florida is hard to beat.

• Scotland

Try coastal courses, or "links", such as the Old Course at St Andrews, Scotland (right) for an entirely different golfing experience. Expect high winds to play havoc with your game.

• Spain

The warm climate of southern Spain has helped create an explosion of golf courses along the Costa del Sol. It is so popular with golfers that it's now nicknamed the "Costa del Golf".

• Dubai

With its sumptuous hotels, great weather, and amazing golf courses, Dubai is becoming increasingly popular as a destination for golfers. Try the perfectly manicured fairways at the Dubai Creek or the Dubai Country Club for a great golf experience.

extreme golf

Like most other sports, golf is constantly evolving and as the popularity of the game grows, so too does the number of weird and wonderful variations. Today, you can play up mountains in Canada, in the deserts of Nevada, and even in the streets of London. So you no longer have to rely upon lush fairways and manicured greens to enjoy a great round of golf.

a

b

c

a Ice golf
Played on the frozen fjords of Uummannaq, Greenland, in March each year, the World Ice Golf Championships attract players from all over the world who compete in temperatures of minus-50°C (using flourescent balls, of course).

b Night golf
Golf is now a 24-hour sport. Floodlit courses are becoming increasingly common, offering golfers the chance to play any time, even when everyone else is asleep.

c Desert golf
In the game of desert golf, golfers take their putts not on greens, but on "browns." This is the tee box of the "Hell Hole" at the annual tournament in Nevada's Black Rock Desert.

golf on the web

As well as reading books and magazines, one of the best places to look for information about golf is on the internet. Here are some useful sites.

GOLF TOURS and ADMINISTRATORS

www.pgatour.com
The home of the United States PGA Tour, featuring full event coverage, statistics, player profiles and instruction.

www.europeantour.com
With all the latest news and results from the European Tour.

www.asianpga.com
The site of the Asian PGA Tour.

www.ladieseuropeantour.com
The online home of women's golf in Europe.

www.lpga.com
The official LPGA site including tournament coverage, news, scores, and golfer biographies.

www.randa.org
The official site of the game's ruling body, the Royal and Ancient.

www.usga.org
The official site of the United States Golf Association, golf's ruling body in America.

TOURNAMENT SITES

www.opengolf.com
www.masters.org
www.usopen.com
www.pga.com
The official sites of the four majors.

ONLINE GOLF MAGAZINES

www.golfdigest.com
The online version of the world's number one golf publication.

www.golfonline.com
Instruction, equipment, and travel from the editors of Golf magazine.

www.golfpunkonline.com
The online version of a fresh and funky golf magazine from the UK.

www.golfinstruction.com
A comprehensive guide to golf tuition for all standards of golfer.

www.learnaboutgolf.com
As the address suggests, this is a great site for those that are new to the game.

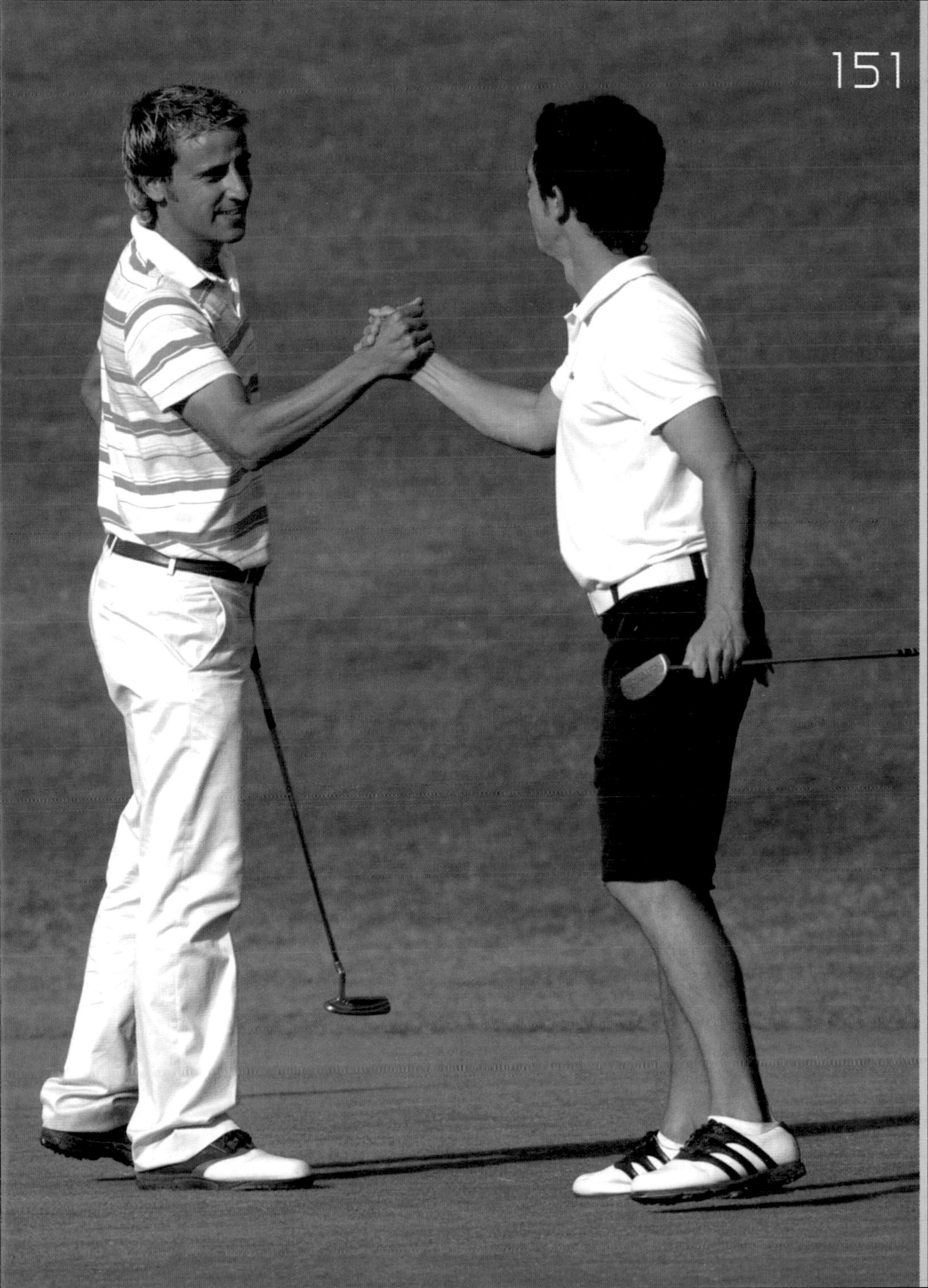

golf talk

Ace – a hole in one.

Address – the stance taken by a player as they prepare to hit the ball.

Air shot – when a player attempts to hit the ball but misses it completely.

Albatross – the British name given to a score of three under par on an individual hole. Known as a "double eagle" in the USA.

Approach shot – normally a short or medium shot played to the putting green.

Apron – the grassy area surrounding the green's putting surface.

Ball in play – the ball is in play as soon as a stroke is made in the tee-off area. It remains in play until the hole is finished except when it is out of bounds, lost, picked up, or when another ball is substituted in accordance with the rules.

Ball marker – a small circular token used to mark the position of the ball when lifting it off the putting green.

Birdie – one stroke under par for a hole.

Bogey – a score of one over par for the hole.

Bump and run – a low chip shot that runs on after landing.

Bunker – a sand-filled hazard.

Caddie (also spelled "**caddy**") – someone who carries a player's clubs during play.

Chip shot – a short approach shot usually hit from near the green.

Choke – to grip further down the club handle.

Club head – the hitting area of a club.

Clubhouse – the main building on a golf course.

Cup – the container in the hole that holds the flagstick in pace.

Dimple – the round indentations on the golf ball cover.

Divot – a piece of turf removed by the club when making a shot. It should always be repaired straight away.

Dogleg – a bend in a fairway.

Dormie – when playing in match play, being as many holes up as there are holes left to play. For example, being five holes up with five holes to play.

Double bogey – a score of two over par for a single hole.

Drain – to sink a putt.

Driving range – an area used for practising.

Drop – the process of putting a ball back in play after it has been declared unplayable or after the ball has been lost.

Eagle – two strokes under par for a single hole.

Face – the hitting area of the club head.

Fairway – the area of the course between the tee and the green that is well-maintained allowing a good lie for the ball.

Fat shot – when the club hits the ground behind the ball prior to impact.

Flier – a ball that is hit without backspin and travels a greater distance than usual.

Follow-through – the final part of the swing following contact with the ball.

Fore – a warning cry to anyone who may be in danger from the flight of the ball.

Fourball – a match in which the better ball of two players is played against the better ball of their opponents.

Foursome – four players playing together. This also refers to a match in which two players play against another pair with each side playing just one ball.

Free drop – a drop when no penalty stroke is incurred.

Fringe – the area surrounding the putting green, which is cut to a height lower than the fairway but not as short as the green itself.

Gimme – a putt so short that is certain to be made on the next shot and will therefore be conceded by an opponent.

Grand Slam – the four major championships: the (British) Open, the US Open, the PGA Championship, and the Masters.

Green – the putting area.

Green fee – the charge made by a course to allow the player to complete a round.

Greenkeeper – the person responsible for the maintenance of the course.

Grip – the part of the shaft that a player holds. Also, the manner in which you hold the club.

Grooves – the linear scoring on a club face.

Grounding the club – placing the club head behind the ball at address.

Halved – when a match is played without a winner emerging. A hole is "halved" when both sides play it in the same number of strokes.

Handicap – the number of strokes by which a player on average exceeds par for a course.

Handicap certificate – a document issued by a player's home club or golfing association that indicates his current handicap.

Hazard – any sand trap, bunker, or water on the golf course that may cause a player difficulty.

Head – the part of the club that makes contact with the ball.

Heel – the part of the club head that is nearest to the shaft.

Hole in one – a hole completed with a single stroke. Also known as an "ace".

Hook – to hit the ball in a manner that causes it to curve from right to left in the case of a right-handed player, or left to right for a left hander.

In – the second nine holes of an 18-hole course, as opposed to "out" – the first nine holes.

Interlocking grip – a grip in which the little finger of the bottom hand is intertwined with the index finger of the top hand.

Jungle – a slang term for heavy rough.

Kick – a term for an erratic bounce.

Lay up – to play a shorter shot than normal instead of going for the green.

Lie – the position of the ball on the ground.

Lip – the rim of the hole or cup.

Local rules – a set of rules for a club determined by the members.

Loft – the angle of the clubface.

Long game – part of the game made up of shots hit with woods and long irons.

Mallet – a putter with a wide and heavy head.

Marker – a small object, such as a coin, that is used to mark the position of a ball when it is lifted off a putting green.

Match play – a competition played with each hole being a separate contest. The team or player winning the most holes is the winner.

Medal play – a competition decided by the lowest overall number of strokes used to complete the round or rounds.

Mulligan – a repeat shot that is allowed to be taken only in friendly play without penalty.

Municipal course – a public course owned by the local government.

Net – a player's final score after he subtracts his handicap.

Nineteenth hole – the nickname for the bar at the clubhouse.

Out – the first nine holes of an 18-hole course. The second nine holes is coming "in".

Out of bounds – the area outside of the course in which play is prohibited. A player is penalized stroke and distance – that is, he must replay the shot with a penalty of one stroke.

Overlapping grip – where the little finger of the bottom hand overlaps the space between the forefinger and second finger of the top hand.

Pairings – groups of two players.

Par – the number of strokes a player should take to complete a round.

Parkland course – a course laid out in grassland with little rough.

Peg – another word for a tee.

Penalty stroke – an additional stroke added to a player's score for an infringement of the rules.

Pick up – to pick up one's ball before holing out. In match play this concedes the hole; in stroke play it incurs disqualification.

Pivot – the rotation of the shoulders, trunk, and hips during a golf swing.

Playing through – passing another group of players who are playing ahead.

Pot bunker – a small sand trap with steep sides.

Preferred lie – local rules which allow a player to improve his lie without penalty.

Provisional ball – a ball played if the previously played ball might be lost or out of bounds.

Pull – a ball that goes to the left of the target when hit by a right-handed player, or to the right for a left hander.

Punch – a low, controlled shot, often played into the wind.

Push – a ball that goes to the right of the target for a right-handed player, or to the left for a left hander

Quitting on the ball – not completing your full swing.

R & A – abbreviation for the Royal and Ancient Golf Club of St. Andrews, Scotland.

Range – see **Driving range**.

Reading the green – judging the path the ball will take across the green on its way to the hole.

Rough – the long grass areas adjacent to fairways and greens.

Run – the distance the ball rolls along the ground once it has landed.

Sand trap – a bunker.

Scratch – a handicap of zero.

Set up – to position yourself for the address.

Shaft – the long section of a club between the grip and the head.

Short game – that part of the game that is made up of chip shots, pitching, and putting.

Skulling – mis-hitting the ball at or above its centre, causing it to travel too far.

Slice – a mis-hit that curves strongly from left to right for the right hander or right to left for the left hander.

Snap-hook – to hit a shot with an acute hook.

Spike mark – a mark made on the green by the cleats of a golf shoe.

Stableford – a method of scoring that uses points instead of strokes.

Stance – a player's position when they are addressing the ball.

Stroke play – a competition in which the total number of strokes for one round, or number of rounds, decides the winner.

Sweet spot – the dead centre of the clubface.

Takeaway – the beginning of the backswing.

Tap in – a very short putt.

Teeing ground – the area in which you must begin each hole.

Three ball – three players playing against each other at the same time.

Threesome – three people playing together, or two playing the same ball against one player.

Top – to hit the ball above its centre causing it to roll or hop along the ground rather than rise.

Touch shot – a delicately hit shot.

Trajectory – the flight path of the ball.

Triple bogey – a score of three-over par on a hole.

Unplayable lie – a lie in which the ball is impossible to play.

Up and down – getting out of trouble or out of a hazard and into the hole in two strokes.

Vardon grip – see **Overlapping grip**.

Waggle – the movement of the club head prior to swinging. A flourishing of the club behind and over the ball.

Winter rules – usually local golf rules that allow players to improve the lie of the ball on the fairway when the ground is in poor condition.

Yips – shakiness or nervousness in making a shot, especially when putting.

index

and finally...

Thanks from the author
I would like to thank: Alcaidesa Links Golf, Costa de la Luz, Spain; San Roque Golf, Cadiz, Spain; Santa Clara Golf Club, Marbella, Spain; Carlos Mena; and Mizuno, for clothing and equipment. Thanks also to froghair (www.froghair.co.uk) and J. Lindberg (www.jlindeberg.com) for their fabulous clothing. Also, thank you to the models, who all worked so hard on the shoot: Carlos Mena Quero, Manuel Arau Jo Duarif, and Ivan Mangas Qrtega.

Thanks for the pictures
133bc Getty, by Andrew Redington; 133b Getty, by Douglas Keister, 140 Getty, by Harry How;141b Getty, by Andrew Redington; 141t Getty, by Donald Miralle; 142 Getty, by Chris McGrath; 143 Stone, by Bob Thomas; 144 Stone, by Bob Krist; 145 Allsport Concepts, by JD Cuban; 146t Panoramic Images; 146b Image Bank, by Larry Dale Gordon; 147 Getty, by Andrew Redington; 148 Getty, by Stuart Franklin; 149t Time & Life Pictures, by John M Burgess; 149b Getty, by Douglas Keister.

Thanks from Dorling Kindersley
DK would like to thank David Summers for editorial asistance and Margaret McCormack for indexing. Also, many thanks to all those who gave their time and provided locations and products for the shoot.
www.alcaidesa.com
www.sanroqueclub.com
www.santaclara-golf.com

About the author
Gavin Newsham is a journalist and writer based in Brighton, England. He is the Associate Editor of the groundbreaking **Golf Punk** magazine and is a regular contributor to the **Observer Sport Monthly** magazine, **The Guardian**, and **The Mail on Sunday**. For his first book, **Letting The Big Dog Eat**, a biography of the American golfer John Daly, he was awarded the Best New Writer Award at the National Sports Book of the Year Awards, 2004.